GREAT BRITONS
LEADERS

Simon Adams

FRANKLIN WATTS
LONDON•SYDNEY

First published in 2007 by
Franklin Watts

Copyright © Franklin
Watts 2007

Franklin Watts
338 Euston Road
London NW1 3BH

Franklin Watts Australia
Level 17/207 Kent Street
Sydney, NSW 2000

A CIP catalogue record for
this book is available from
the British Library.

Dewey number: 920.02

ISBN: 978 0 7496 7476 2

Printed in China

Franklin Watts is a division
of Hachette Children's
Books.

Designer: Thomas Keenes
Art Director: Jonathan Hair
Editor: Sarah Ridley
Editor-in-Chief:
John C. Miles
Picture Research:
Diana Morris

Picture credits:
Art Media/HIP/Topfoto: 31.
Fortean Picture Library/
Topfoto: 17. HIP/Topfoto:
13, 19, 20, 23, 33.
Houghton/Topfoto: 15.
Picturepoint/Topham: 9,
24, 27, 37, 39, 42.
Roger-Viollet/Topham: 35.
Ann Ronan Picture Library/
HIP/Topfoto: 10. Topfoto:
front cover, 28, 41. UPP/
Topfoto: 45. Charles
Walker/Topfoto: 6.

Every attempt has been made to
clear copyright. Should there be
any inadvertent omission please
apply to the publisher for
rectification.

CONTENTS

INTRODUCTION

O ver the course of their long history, the people of Britain have been led by some remarkable people. Some of its kings, queens, military leaders, freedom fighters and politicians are among the most famous people in history, known throughout Europe and the rest of the world. Yet Britain has also had its fair share of useless monarchs and incompetent or corrupt politicians, and at times has been led very badly indeed.

It is very difficult to say exactly what makes a good leader but, in their own way, each of these 20 men and women has made a massive contribution to the history of this island. David Lloyd George and Winston Churchill led Britain to victory in the two world wars while the Duke of Marlborough and Horatio Nelson won important battles against the French. Queen Victoria ruled over the biggest empire the world has ever known.

Some of the people in this book come from the regions of Britain: Boudica was an ancient Briton who inspired her people in their fight against the Roman invaders; Robert Bruce was a Scot who led his countrymen to independence from England; while Owain Glyndwr was a Welsh prince who tried, but failed, to gain independence for Wales.

Many of the kings and queens in this book were, of course, monarchs of England only, as Wales did not become part of England until the 1280s and the crowns of Scotland and England did not unite until 1603.

Finally, the 20 men and women in this book were all born or brought up in Britain. Excluded, therefore, are those great leaders, such as Canute or William the Conqueror, who were born abroad or who were foreigners to this country. Also excluded are Irish leaders, as most of their country is now independent from Britain.

You, of course, will have your own favourite leaders, and will wonder why some of them are not in this book. A list such as this is always personal, and can always be changed with good reason. But it is true to say that each and every person in this book changed the course of British history in one way or another, and has left their mark for future generations to study, and admire.

BOUDICA
QUEEN OF THE ICENI

BORN Norfolk?, c. 30 CE
REIGNED 60–61 CE
DIED West Midlands?, 61 CE
AGE About 31 years

It is unfortunate that we know so little about Boudica, for she was obviously a very remarkable woman. Had she won against the Romans, the history of Britain might have been very different indeed.

This 19th-century bronze statue of Boudica and her daughters riding in a war chariot stands on the Victoria Embankment in London.

Boudica or Boudicca – also known as Boadicea – was the wife of Prasutagus, king of the powerful Iceni tribe of Norfolk. After the Romans invaded and occupied England in 43 CE, they organised the tribes that lived alongside them into a series of dependent kingdoms. The tribes kept control of their own affairs but the Romans remained in overall charge. At first this system worked well, but in 60 CE Prasutagus died.

The Romans then decided to end Iceni independence and make them part of Roman Britain. However, the Roman official managing the take-over brutally mistreated Boudica, her daughters and many other Iceni. Led by Boudica, the Iceni rose in revolt. Joined by the nearby Trinovantes tribe, Boudica marched south from her capital outside Norwich, wiping out a force of Roman footsoldiers on the way. Her troops first destroyed the important Roman city of Colchester and then marched on to attack London and St Albans as well.

According to the Roman historian Tacitus, casualties on both sides were huge, with whole towns razed to the ground. He described events in Britain as a *clades* (disaster), for the Romans were about to lose control of their newly won lands to a fearsome opponent.

While all this was going on, the Roman governor, Suetonius Paullinus, was away fighting in Wales. He rushed back towards London and met Boudica somewhere in the West Midlands. Although Boudica's army was bigger, the more professional Romans won. Boudica escaped but died shortly afterwards, probably by taking poison. The Romans then went on to conquer all of England and Wales.

Had Boudica succeeded in her revolt, Britain would have been one of the few countries in Europe to defeat the Romans and throw them out for good. 🇬🇧

Caratacus

The most important British leader to fight the invading Romans from 43 CE onwards was **CARATACUS**, son of King Cunobelin of the Catuvellauni tribe of southeast England. After a Roman army defeated him, Caratacus continued to fight on, probably in the mountains of Wales. He reappeared in 47 CE, leading a rebel army but, once again, he was defeated. In 51 CE he was captured and handed over to the Romans by Queen Cartimandua of the Brigantes. Caratacus was taken to Rome where, according to Tacitus, he made a speech that so impressed Emperor Claudius that he was granted his freedom rather than be executed.

ALFRED THE GREAT
'KING OF ALL ENGLAND'

BORN Wantage, Oxfordshire, 846 or 849
REIGNED 871–899
DIED Winchester, Hampshire, October 899
AGE 50 or 53 years

Alfred is the only English king to be called 'the Great', and he thoroughly deserves this title. As one writer at the time said: 'The aim of all his work was to promote the good of his people.'

Alfred was the fifth and youngest son of King Aethelwulf of Wessex, an independent kingdom in southern England. In 871 he succeeded his brother Aethelred as king. At the time, Wessex was threatened by constant Danish invasions. In January 878 the Danes made a surprise attack, forcing Alfred to seek refuge in the Somerset marshes. While in hiding, a story is told that he stayed in a swineherd's cottage.

There he let some cakes burn that he was meant to be watching. The swineherd's wife told him off, but was horrified to then discover that her lodger was, in fact, her king. Unfortunately this popular story is now believed by historians to be only a legend. Alfred then gathered an army together and defeated the Danes at Ethandune in May 878. He pursued them back to their camp near Bath and surrounded them. He could

The *Anglo-Saxon Chronicle*

In 891 Alfred asked some monks to compile a written history of England. Written in Anglo-Saxon, the language of the people, rather than Latin, the language of the Church, the *Anglo-Saxon Chronicle* kept a year-by-year record of events in England from the end of the Roman occupation in the 400s right up to 1154, when the monks of Peterborough Abbey made the last entry. Among the kings it mentions is **ECGBEHRT**, Alfred's grandfather and King of Wessex from 802–839, who in 829 was the first to be acknowledged by his fellow English kings as 'King of all England', although in reality he was England's king in name only.

This miniature enamel portrait of Alfred is inscribed around the edge, Aelfred me ech eh t gewyrcan – 'Alfred ordered me to be made'.

have killed them all, but decided to be merciful, insisting only that their leader, Guthrum, be baptised a Christian with Alfred as his godfather. Alfred and the Danes then divided England between them, with Alfred overseeing both halves.

In 886 battle resumed again. Alfred captured London and was recognised by both English and Danes as 'King of all England'. To secure his kingdom, he built numerous fortresses or *burhs* – the Saxon word from which we get 'borough', or 'town'. He set up a rota system for military service so that he always had a trained army but its members could get on with farming or other jobs when not needed. In addition, he built a fleet of warships to stop new Danish armies landing in England, which is why he is known as the 'father of the English Navy'.

As if this is not enough, Alfred reformed all the laws and wrote them down so that they could be properly understood. He also kept detailed records of his new kingdom, and encouraged learning and the arts.

RICHARD I
'THE LIONHEART'

BORN Beaumont Palace, Oxford, 8 September 1157
REIGNED 1189–1199
DIED Châlus, France, 6 April 1199
AGE 41 years

King for only ten years, Richard is one of England's most famous monarchs, remembered for his military campaigns in the Holy Land and for his love of gallantry. Yet, he was in England for only seven months during his entire reign, and almost bankrupted his country.

A 19th-century impression of Richard and his knights landing in the Holy Land.

The Plantagenets

Richard I was a member of the Plantagenet family that ruled England from 1154 until 1399. His father, **HENRY II** (reigned 1154–1189), ruled an empire that included much of France, as well as England and Ireland.

Richard's brother and successor, **JOHN** (reigned 1199–1216), lost almost all the French lands and was forced to sign an agreement known as the *Magna Carta* ('Great Charter') with his nobles. This charter restricted royal power and, among other things, stated that no free man should be arrested or imprisoned except by the laws of the land.

During the reign of John's son, **HENRY III** (reigned 1216–1272), parliament as we know it today began to form, with representatives summoned to attend.

As soon as he became king, Richard sold state and Church lands and offices to pay for a crusade (holy war) to free the Holy Land from Muslim control. Once he arrived, Richard captured the important city of Acre in 1291 and defeated the Muslim ruler, Saladin, in battle, forcing him to allow Christians to make pilgrimages (religious journeys) to Jerusalem without fear of attack. His success in battle and enormous personal courage gave him the name *Coeur de Lion* – French for 'Lionheart' – and he became famous across Europe.

While he was away, Richard married Berengaria of Navarre, a marriage negotiated by Richard's mother, Eleanor of Aquitaine. The marriage took place on the island of Cyprus, one of the most unlikely places for the wedding of an English king. Berengaria was actually crowned Queen of England and Cyprus.

Richard was returning home when he was captured in 1292 by the Duke of Austria and handed over to Henry VI, Emperor of Germany. Henry VI demanded a huge ransom (payment) for Richard's safe release. Back in England, every Englishman had to pay a quarter of his annual income to raise enough money to release Richard in 1294.

Once back home, Richard was crowned for the second time to show his power before he set off once more, this time for France. He wanted to regain those lands and castles that had been lost to King Philip IV of France while he had been fighting in the Holy Land. This time he did not return, dying after he was hit by an arrow while besieging the castle of Châlus. On his deathbed, Richard pardoned the captured archer, Bertram, gave him a hundred shillings and set him free.

EDWARD I
'HAMMER OF THE SCOTS'

BORN Palace of
Westminster, London,
17 or 18 June 1239
REIGNED 1272–1307
DIED Burgh-on-Sands,
Cumbria, 7 July 1307
AGE 68 years

Without a doubt, Edward I was one of the most able and outstanding kings of England. He tried and almost succeeded in creating a united kingdom of England, Scotland, Wales and Ireland, and transformed the government and laws of England.

When Edward became king in 1272, he was on crusade in the Holy Land and only returned home to be crowned in 1274. Edward was overlord of (had power over) both Ireland and Wales, but after Prince Llywelyn of Wales refused to accept this, Edward invaded Wales. He defeated Llywelyn in 1282 and joined Wales with England in 1284.

Edward then turned his attention to Scotland, invading in 1296 and again in 1298 to claim power over Scotland. When Robert Bruce (see pages 14-15) took over the leadership of the Scottish resistance to English rule and had himself crowned king in 1306, Edward headed north again, only to die in Cumbria before he could reach the border. Not for nothing was Edward known as the 'Hammer of the Scots'.

Aside from his military campaigns, Edward was also a great ruler, genuinely wanting to bring law, order and prosperity to his kingdom. Between 1275 and 1290 he introduced reforms that ended quarrels over land ownership, controlled highway robbery and violence by appointing the first justices of the peace, and gave local communities responsibility to police themselves. Most importantly, in 1295 he summoned what has become known as the Model Parliament: each county, city and important town sent two representatives each to parliament, in effect creating an early system of representative democracy.

Princes of Wales

While Edward was campaigning in Wales in 1284, his wife Eleanor gave birth to a son and heir, Edward (the future Edward II), at Caernarfon Castle. In 1301 Edward gave his son the title of Prince of Wales, a title which has been given to every male heir to the throne ever since. There have been 21 Princes of Wales in total, including the current titleholder, Prince Charles, although seven of them died before they became king. Only two – the future Edward VIII and Prince Charles – were invested (created) in Caernarfon Castle, the rest in London.

Caernarfon Castle in North Wales, built by Edward I.

ROBERT BRUCE
THE GREATEST SCOTSMAN

BORN Probably near Chelmsford, Essex, 11 July 1274
REIGNED 1306–1329
DIED Cardross Castle, Dumbartonshire, 7 June 1329
AGE 54 years

When the seven-year-old Queen Margaret died in 1290, the Scottish nobles were unable to pick a successor and asked Edward I of England to choose. As a result, England constantly interferred in Scottish affairs, something that Robert Bruce successfully challenged.

Although born in England, Robert Bruce came from a Scottish family. At first he supported Edward I but later he joined a revolt against him, led by William Wallace. After Wallace's death, Bruce was the ideal man to take up the cause of Scottish independence.

In 1306 Bruce was crowned King of Scotland at Scone Abbey in Perthshire.

A year later, Edward I died before he could invade Scotland again. However, this did not solve Bruce's problems as there were already English troops in Scotland, searching for him. He went into hiding for several years while he raised an army to fight the English.

In 1314 Bruce's army was strong enough to besiege Stirling Castle, one of the

Scottish kings

Like England, Scotland has had its fair share of good, and bad, kings. In 849 **KENNETH MACALPIN**, King of the Scots (died 859), defeated the Picts to become the first king of a united Scotland north of the River Forth. **MALCOLM II** (reigned 1015–34) brought southern Scotland into the kingdom in 1018. One of his successors was **MACBETH** (1040–57), an able ruler, not the murderous king of Shakespeare's play. **ALEXANDER II** (1214–49) agreed roughly the current border with England in 1237, while **ALEXANDER III** (1249–86) gained the Western Isles from Norway in 1266. In 1469 **JAMES III** (1460–88) finally acquired Orkney and Shetland from Norway, giving Scotland the boundaries it has today.

main English-held fortresses. The new, weak English king, Edward II, tried to lift the siege but was decisively defeated just south of the castle at Bannockburn. Bruce now expected the English to leave Scotland alone, but when they failed to do so, a group of Scottish lords and bishops met at Arbroath in 1320 and sent a letter to Pope John XXII, asking him to recognise Scottish independence:

'For, as long as a hundred of us remain alive, never will we on any conditions be subjected to the lordship of the English. It is in truth not for glory, ... that we are fighting, but for freedom alone.'

In 1323 England and Scotland agreed a truce and, after more fighting, finally signed a peace treaty in 1328. Unfortunately, Bruce died the next year and England continued to claim the throne of Scotland. 🏴

This statue of Robert Bruce stands at Bannockburn, scene of his greatest victory over the English.

OWAIN GLYNDWR
WELSH RESISTANCE LEADER

BORN North Wales, 1359
DIED Possibly Herefordshire, c.1416
AGE About 57 years

After the death of Prince Llywelyn in 1282 (see page 12), the Welsh never lost hope that one day they might regain their independence from England. Their best hope came with Owain Glyndwr, a descendant of the ancient Welsh princes of Powys and Dyfed.

Glyndwr was born into a wealthy Anglo-Welsh family. As a young man, he supported Richard II as his king. But, in 1399, Henry Bolingbroke took the throne from his cousin Richard and declared himself King Henry IV. Glyndwr was in dispute with a neighbour about his land and appealed to parliament for help. The neighbour, a good friend of Henry, used his influence to get the appeal rejected and withheld a summons from the king for Glyndwr to join his army. By failing to respond, Glyndwr had committed treason.

So, on 16 September 1400, Glyndwr rose in revolt against Henry IV. His followers named him 'Prince Owain IV of Wales' and the revolt spread as he seized towns and castles across Wales. He even attracted support from abroad, with the French sending a small army in 1403 and again in 1405.

Henry IV was in no real position to deal with the Welsh, as he had trouble in England with another revolt led by the powerful Percy family. Owain Glyndwr took the opportunity to summon a Welsh parliament, which met at Machynlleth in 1404 and again the next year in Harlech Castle. He appeared to be sweeping all before him until the English began to blockade the rebels, which stopped them from getting enough food and other supplies.

By 1407 the rebellion was nearing its end. Glyndwr continued to fight a guerrilla war, but after 1412 he disappeared, probably dying in 1416. A contemporary record reveals that, 'Very many said that he died; the seers [wise men] maintain he did not.' Like King Arthur, Owain Glyndwr lives on in the imagination.

This image of Owain Glyndwr is taken from the large wax seal fixed to his official documents.

HENRY V
VICTOR OF AGINCOURT

BORN Monmouth
Castle, 9 August or
16 September 1387
REIGNED 1413–1422
DIED Bois-de-Vincennes
Castle, France,
1 September 1422
AGE 34 or 35 years

Henry V continues to excite and inspire us almost 500 years after his death. A tear-away child who would rather drink and gamble than behave himself at court, he became a king whose reputation quickly spread across Europe as one of the finest soldiers of his day.

When Henry became king in 1413, the Hundred Years' War with France had already been going on for 76 years, and early English gains had largely been lost to the French. Henry renewed England's claim to the French throne and in 1415 set off for France, winning the northern port of Harfleur after a five-week siege. His exhausted army of 6,000 soldiers, mainly archers and foot-soldiers, then marched across Normandy to face a vast 36,000-strong French army at Agincourt. The French cavalry charged straight at the English, but were mown

Late medieval kings

The greatest of English kings during the late medieval period was **EDWARD III** (reigned 1327–77). Edward started the Hundred Years' War against France – which actually lasted on and off for 116 years – when he laid claim to the French throne in 1337. His son, **EDWARD THE BLACK PRINCE** (1330–76), won numerous victories, notably at Crécy (1346) and Poitiers (1356).

After the not very successful reign of **RICHARD II** (1377–99), two rival branches of the ruling Plantagenet family fought for the throne during the Wars of the Roses. The Lancastrians, who fought under the badge of a red rose, ran the country from 1399 to 1461. Then the Yorkists, who used a white rose as their badge, took control until 1485. Notable kings at this period include **EDWARD IV** (1461–83), who brought peace and wealth to the country, and **RICHARD III** (1483–85), who had many untrue stories told about him, perhaps because he finally lost the throne to the Tudors.

down by the English archers; 18,000 Frenchmen lost their lives or were seriously injured and at least 1,000 were captured while English casualties amounted to fewer than 200.

Henry returned to England triumphant, and in 1417 went back to France again to conquer Normandy. In 1420 Charles VI of France signed the Treaty of Troyes with Henry making him regent (governor) of France and heir to his throne. In June that year, Henry married Catherine of Valois, Charles's daughter. The way was now open for Henry to inherit the French throne, but in 1422, while fighting in France, he caught dysentery and died. Had he lived, the history of England and France might have been quite different.

This portrait of Henry shows him as a sensitive and thoughtful young man, although he was a headstrong and adventurous king.

HENRY VIII
THE MUCH-MARRIED KING

BORN Greenwich
Palace, Kent,
28 June 1491
REIGNED 1509–47
DIED Whitehall Palace,
London,
28 January 1547
AGE 55 years

One of the most famous kings of England, Henry VIII started his reign as a handsome young man of culture and learning but ended it as an overweight, cruel tyrant. He had transformed his country but at huge cost to his subjects.

Henry was a tall, fair and handsome man, although in later life he became very overweight.

When Henry became king in 1509, he left affairs in the hands of his main advisor, Cardinal Thomas Wolsey. At this time, Henry was still a devout Catholic. When he defended the Church against the writings of the German reformer Martin Luther, the Pope gave him the title 'Defender of the Faith', a title still used by British monarchs today.

But, in 1529, when Thomas Wolsey failed to persuade the Pope to grant the divorce Henry wanted from his wife, Catherine of Aragon, he charged Wolsey with treason and took matters into his own hands. He got his marriage annulled (cancelled) and, in 1534, he declared himself Supreme Head of the Church of England. He broke away from the Pope, the head of the Roman Catholic Church in Rome. In addition, he ordered the Bible to be translated into English so that everyone could read it, and started England on the course to become a Protestant rather than a Catholic nation. In 1536–39 he seized the land and buildings of the monasteries for himself and closed them down.

Meanwhile, on the military side, Henry paid for many new ships to increase the size of the English Navy. He fought expensive wars against France and twice defeated an invading Scottish army, killing most of the Scottish nobility in the process. He finally officially joined Wales to England and in 1541 Henry declared himself king rather than overlord of Ireland. Opposition to his rule was great, with several major rebellions during his reign. By the end of his life, Henry had ordered the death of at least one member of about 50,000 English families. 🇬🇧

The six wives

Henry holds the record as the most-married English king. His first wife, **CATHERINE OF ARAGON** (1485–1536), was the widow of his oldest brother, Arthur. They married in 1509 and had one daughter, Mary, in 1516, but Henry had the marriage annulled in 1533 because she failed to produce a male heir. That same year he married **ANNE BOLEYN** (c.1501–36), who gave birth to his second daughter, Elizabeth. Henry soon lost interest in Anne and had her executed for high treason in 1536. Soon after he married **JANE SEYMOUR** (c.1509–37), who died after giving birth to a son, Edward. In January 1540 he married a German princess, **ANNE OF CLEVES** (1515–57), but that marriage soon failed. Later that year, he married **CATHERINE HOWARD** (c.1525–42), but she had a series of young lovers and was soon executed for treason. His sixth wife, **CATHERINE PARR** (c.1512–48), had already been married twice before, but after they married in 1543, she became an ideal stepmother to his three children.

ELIZABETH I
'GOOD QUEEN BESS'

BORN Greenwich
Palace, Kent,
7 September 1533
REIGNED 1558–1603
DIED Richmond Palace,
Surrey,
24 March 1603
AGE 69 years

Today many people consider Elizabeth I to be one of England's most successful monarchs, the 'Virgin Queen' who ruled over a glittering court. Yet she had to overcome enormous challenges before she came to the throne, and struggled to stay there against plots and invasions.

Elizabeth was just 25 when she became queen on the death of her sister, Mary I. Mary was a Roman Catholic who had tried to undo the religious changes of Henry VIII and Edward VI and take England back to the Roman Catholic faith. Elizabeth, however, was Protestant, and reintroduced a moderate form of Protestantism that is the basis of the Church of England today. Elizabeth's Protestantism, however, made her many enemies abroad, notably the Catholic Philip II of Spain. When Elizabeth began to help his Protestant Dutch subjects rebel against his rule, Philip decided to support Catholic plots against Elizabeth. He wanted to replace Elizabeth with her cousin, the Catholic Mary Queen of Scots, who had fled Scotland in 1568,

Her troubled early life

Elizabeth was the second daughter of **HENRY VIII** (reigned 1509–47) but was less than three years old when her mother, **ANNE BOLEYN** (c.1501–36), was executed for treason. Within days, Elizabeth was declared illegitimate and removed from the succession to the throne. Reinstated to the succession by her father in 1544 as third in line after her brother **EDWARD VI** (reigned 1547–53) and older sister **MARY I** (1553–58), she almost lost her life when Mary sent her to the Tower of London in 1554 on suspicion of treason. Released after two months, she was then put under house arrest and remained under constant supervision until Mary died. It is little wonder that she refused to marry, stating that she was 'married to England'.

The many portraits of Elizabeth painted during her reign show her as an attractive and intelligent woman.

and had been kept prisoner by Elizabeth ever since. When Mary became involved in a plot to assassinate Elizabeth and make Mary queen instead, Elizabeth put her on trial and had her executed for treason in 1587.

In response, Philip sent an Armada, a vast fleet of ships, to invade England in 1588. But bad weather and the clever actions of the English saw the Armada off, at a great loss of Spanish life and prestige.

Elizabeth was good at making speeches, which she wrote herself. Addressing English troops ready to fight off the Armada, she said: 'I know I have the body of a weak and feeble woman, but I have the heart and stomach of a king, and of a king of England too.'

Such words help to explain why she was so loved and admired by her people.

OLIVER CROMWELL
LORD PROTECTOR OF ENGLAND

BORN Huntingdon,
25 April 1599
HEAD OF STATE
1649–58
DIED Whitehall,
London,
3 September 1658
AGE 59 years

The son of a Huntingdon landowner who entered parliament in 1628, there was little about Oliver Cromwell to mark him out in any way. Yet he rose to become an inspired military leader and the head of the first and only republic in British history.

Cromwell was not a handsome man, although an enemy described him as 'of majestic deportment and comely presence.'

When civil war broke out in England in 1642 between King Charles I and parliament, Oliver Cromwell supported parliament's side by leading an armed force. He was so successful that when, in 1645, parliament decided to merge all its existing armies and militias into a single fighting force known as the New Model Army, Cromwell was appointed second-in-command. With victory in sight in 1647, Cromwell tried to come to an agreement with Charles I. When that failed, he once again took up arms. Reluctantly, he agreed that the only way to end the civil war was to get rid of the king.

After Charles I was executed in 1649, parliament set up a Council of State with Oliver Cromwell at its head, and declared England and Wales to be a 'Commonwealth and free state', or a republic. Cromwell then moved to crush Irish resistance in 1649 and defeat an invading Scottish army in 1651, bringing both these kingdoms into the republic as well.

Cromwell was now at the height of his powers, but was unable to create a system of government that had support from both the people and the army. In 1653 he expelled the existing parliament and set up a new one, known as the Barebones Parliament after one of its members. Its members were put forward by the army and represented all four

The Wars of the Three Kingdoms

CHARLES I (reigned 1625–49) was king of three kingdoms: England, Scotland and Ireland, each with its own parliament, religion and laws. Charles believed that he had a divine (god-given) right to rule, but his religious policies caused rebellion in Scotland in 1638 and Ireland in 1641. When Charles tried to arrest five members of the English parliament in 1642, civil war broke out in England too. Charles, however, was a stubborn man who refused to back down. The English parliament accused him of having 'levied and maintained a cruel war in the land'. For this, Charles was executed outside Whitehall Palace in London on 30 January 1649.

parts of the country, making it the first true parliament of the British Isles.

When the Barebones Parliament broke down in December 1653, Cromwell made himself Lord Protector supported by a small parliament. This too, was less than successful, but when some members of parliament wanted to make him king in 1657, Cromwell refused. Worn out, he died the following year, an honourable man who had tried to make sense and order out of the chaos he found around him.

THE DUKE OF MARLBOROUGH
BRITAIN'S GREATEST MILITARY GENIUS

John Churchill, the 1st Duke of Marlborough, is considered to be the greatest military genius in British history. The historian Sir Edward Creasy wrote that he, '... never fought a battle that he did not win, and never besieged a place that he did not take.'

Churchill was born into a wealthy family in southwest England. At the age of 17 he became a soldier for James, Charles II's brother and heir to the throne. He fought in the Mediterranean and the Netherlands, gaining useful experience each time.

In 1685 James became king but quickly faced a rebellion led by Charles's illegitimate son, the Duke of Monmouth. Churchill was promoted to major-general and played an important role in putting the rebellion down. As a Roman Catholic, James II was not popular with everyone. In 1688 seven leading statesmen asked James's Protestant son-in-law, William of Orange, to take over the throne. At first Churchill supported James, but soon changed sides, taking the army with him. Churchill now served the new King William III.

William rewarded Churchill with the earldom of Marlborough, but although he fought for William against the French and Irish, he was not entirely trusted by the new king. In 1692 he was publicly disgraced when it was discovered that he was in secret contact with the exiled James II. For a time Churchill lived abroad as governor of the Hudson's Bay Company in Canada.

In 1702 William died and was succeeded by his sister-in-law, Anne. When war broke out against the French in 1702 to stop Louis XIV taking over the Spanish throne and dominating Europe, Anne made Churchill Captain-General of the English troops and Commander-in-Chief of the European armies fighting France. After a series of successes, Churchill became the Duke of Marlborough. He was a clever and energetic commander, always securing the best positions for his troops to fight from and attacking the enemy when it was least expected. He made sure his troops were well fed and supplied, and always led them into battle himself.

A series of great victories followed, notably Blenheim (1704), which saved Austria from invasion, Ramillies (1706), which expelled the French from the Netherlands, and Oudenarde (1708) and Malplaquet (1709), two massive victories against bigger French armies. In 1710, however, a new government in London began to negotiate a peace treaty with the French, eventually signed at Utrecht in 1713. Meanwhile Churchill was accused of corruption in 1711 and relieved of his command. He retired and spent his remaining days building his vast new home at Blenheim, outside Oxford. His distant successor was Britain's wartime prime minister, Winston Churchill (see pages 40-41).

The Duke of Marlborough was a brilliant military commander who led a multinational force drawn from many European nations.

27

ROBERT WALPOLE
BRITAIN'S FIRST PRIME MINISTER

BORN Houghton Hall, Norfolk, 28 August 1676
PRIME MINISTER 1721–42
DIED London, 18 March 1745
AGE 68 years

Robert Walpole was Britain's first Prime Minister, holding the job for almost 21 years. In 1732 George II gave him 10 Downing Street, which remains the official home of the Prime Minister in London.

Robert Walpole was a good-natured, cheerful and tolerant man who had great political skills.

Walpole was the son of a Norfolk landowner who supported the Whigs, one of the two main political parties in parliament. The Whigs supported Queen Anne and the Protestant succession to the throne while the other main party, the Tories, supported the exiled Catholic king, James II.

Walpole entered parliament in 1701 and quickly rose to power, becoming Secretary of State for War in 1708. However the Tories won power in 1710 and accused Walpole of corruption, sending him to the Tower of London for six months in 1712.

Walpole's future looked bleak, but in 1714 Queen Anne died and was replaced by the German-born king, George I. He distrusted the Tories because they had not wanted him to become king. The Whigs returned to power and Walpole became First Lord of the Treasury in 1715. Out of office again from 1717–20, he returned to government just as a major financial scandal broke. Many of his colleagues were found guilty of corruption and had to resign, but Walpole was unaffected by the scandal.

In April 1721 Walpole was appointed First Lord of the Treasury, Chancellor of the Exchequer and Leader of the House of Commons, sharing power in government with Lord Townshend, who sat in the House of Lords. The two ran

The Prime Minister

During the reign of **CHARLES II** (1660–85), the king began to consult a few important ministers in his private cabinet or apartments. By the time of **WILLIAM III** (1688–1702), this 'cabinet' of ministers ran the government and held weekly meetings led by the king. When **GEORGE I** (1714–27) became king, this had to change as he could not speak English. George I asked Walpole to lead the cabinet as his Prime, or First, Minister.

the government together until 1730, when Walpole became the unchallenged leader of the government and the king's Prime or First Minister until his resignation in 1742.

Walpole was a great political and financial manager who, by keeping the country largely at peace, greatly increased the country's wealth. He made sure that the new Hanoverian dynasty of George I and his successors held on to the British throne and built up the Whigs into the strongest party in British politics for half a century.

HORATIO NELSON
HERO OF TRAFALGAR

BORN Burnham
Thorpe, Norfolk, 29
September 1758
DIED Off Cape
Trafalgar, Spain, 21
October 1805
AGE 47 years

Horatio Nelson is Britain's most successful naval commander, famous for his defeat of Napoleon and the French at the Battle of Trafalgar, and for the loss of both his right eye and right arm in combat.

Nelson was the son of an Anglican clergyman and joined the navy at the age of 12. He first commanded a ship during the American War of Independence (1775–83) but rose to fame during the wars against France (1793–1815).

He played an important role in the defeat of the French at Cape St Vincent in 1797 where, having already lost his eye in 1794, he was severely wounded in the chest. Some months later he then lost his right arm during a failed attack on Santa Cruz in Tenerife. In 1798 he led the fleet that destroyed the French at Aboukir Bay off the coast of Egypt, ending the French Emperor Napoleon's hopes of invading that country. Yet again he was severely wounded, this time in the head.

Once he had recovered, he commanded the fleet that destroyed the Danes (France's political friends) at Copenhagen in 1801. After a brief period of peace

The Duke of Wellington

While Nelson was defeating the French at sea, **SIR ARTHUR WELLESLEY** (1769–1852) was doing it on land. He made his name fighting in India (1797–1805) and then against Napoleon and the French in the Peninsular War in Spain (1808–14), eventually invading France itself and forcing Napoleon to abdicate in 1814. In 1814 Wellesley was rewarded with the title of Duke of Wellington. When Napoleon returned from exile, Wellington commanded the British forces that, with the Prussians, finally defeated Napoleon at Waterloo in 1815. A national hero, Wellington twice became Prime Minister.

This full-length portrait of Nelson was painted by Sir William Beechey in 1807, shortly after Nelson's death.

between Britain and France in 1802–03, war broke out again. Nelson took command of the Mediterranean fleet, with the job of preventing the French fleet from leaving its main Mediterranean base at Toulon. When the fleet sailed out into the Atlantic to attack British shipping in April 1805, Nelson chased it across the Atlantic Ocean to the West Indies and back again.

By now, the French had linked up with a Spanish fleet. Nelson, in command on board HMS *Victory*, met the French and the Spanish off the coast of Cape Trafalgar in October 1805. The Royal Navy smashed the combined fleet, proving once and for all Britain's superior seapower. During the battle, Nelson was wounded and died. Many of his men wept on hearing of his death. An exceptional naval leader who made clever battle plans, he was not afraid to take risks in order to win a battle.

QUEEN VICTORIA
'THE GRANDMOTHER OF EUROPE'

BORN Kensington Palace, London, 24 May 1819
REIGNED 1837–1901
DIED Osborne House, Isle of Wight, 22 January 1901
AGE 81 years

Queen Victoria ruled for 63 years, longer than any other British king or queen. She made the monarchy popular again and brought stability to the nation. During her reign Britain became the industrial powerhouse of the world and its empire the largest the world had ever seen.

Victoria was only 18 when she came to the throne. She was a headstrong, independent young woman, totally convinced that she was always right.

In 1840 she married her German cousin, Prince Albert of Saxe-Coburg-Gotha, and came to rely on him for advice and support. They had nine children, who later married into all the important royal families of Europe. By the time of her death, Victoria was grandmother to almost every European monarch.

In 1861 Albert died of typhus and Victoria was devastated. She went into permanent mourning, and for 13 years was never seen in public, reading all official papers in her private rooms. In 1874 she began to go out in public

Victoria's predecessors

Victoria's grandfather, **GEORGE III** (reigned 1760–1820), was a diligent ruler whose last years were marked by a disease that made him appear mad. In 1811, his son George was made Prince Regent and ruled for his father.

GEORGE IV (1820–30) had numerous mistresses and one secret wife. His official marriage in 1795 to Caroline of Brunswick was a disaster and they soon parted. Their only child died in childbirth. He was not popular.

His brother, **WILLIAM IV** (1830–37), never expected to become king. He had already had ten children with an actress before his coronation. Many thought he was not fit for the job, yet he was a popular ruler. He was Queen Victoria's uncle.

again, encouraged by Prime Minister Benjamin Disraeli (see pages 34–35). Her Golden Jubilee in 1887, and her Diamond Jubilee ten years later, showed how popular she was as a queen. She was mourned by the whole nation when she died in 1901.

Although parliament governed the country, Victoria had some very strong opinions of her own which she often expressed to her ministers. Her devotion to duty, her strong sense of what was right, and her role as a mother-figure for the nation and the Empire meant that she single-handedly wrote the job description of how a monarch of a modern, democratic nation should act. 🇬🇧

Queen Victoria with her three descendants: Edward VII (left, reigned 1901–10), George V (right, 1910–36) and the infant Edward VIII (reigned 1936).

BENJAMIN DISRAELI
'TO THE TOP OF THE GREASY POLE'

BORN London,
21 December 1804
PRIME MINISTER 1868,
1874–80
DIED London,
19 April 1881
AGE 76 years

Benjamin Disraeli, the son of a Jewish writer, was brought up as a Christian and wrote political novels before he entered parliament. He finally rose, '... to the top of the greasy pole...' (in his own words) to become one of the best prime ministers of the 19th century.

Disraeli entered parliament as a Conservative (Tory) in 1837, and gave a disastrous first speech. He was left out of Sir Robert Peel's Conservative government in 1841, after which he often opposed Peel and helped to remove him from power in 1846. The Conservative Party then split in two, and Disraeli emerged as the co-leader of Peel's opponents alongside Lord Derby. In 1852 and again in 1858–59, Derby became Prime Minister with Disraeli as Chancellor of the Exchequer, but both governments quickly collapsed.

In 1866 Derby and Disraeli were back in power. Disraeli introduced a Reform Act that increased the number of middle- and skilled working-class men who could vote. He hoped this would benefit the Conservative Party, but when he finally became Prime Minister in 1868, he survived in office for less than a year before he was defeated by the Liberals.

In 1874 Disraeli returned to power. He spent the next six years in government making changes which improved the lives of poorer people in Britain. There were acts to improve working conditions, housing, public health and education. He did much to promote the British Empire, making Queen Victoria Empress of India in 1876. Queen Victoria liked Disraeli and made him 1st Earl of Beaconsfield in 1876. He was defeated by William Gladstone (see pages 36-37) in the 1880 general election.

Disraeli's importance was to tie the upper and working classes together in 'one nation' by keeping the institutions of the country, like the monarchy, intact while at the same time introducing social reforms. He therefore helped to make the Conservative Party the most successful in British history. It held office for 73 out of the 130 years between 1867 and its defeat in 1997.

Disraeli was a flamboyant figure who made his Conservative Party the most electorally successful political party in British history.

WILLIAM GLADSTONE
THE 'GRAND OLD MAN'

BORN Liverpool,
29 December 1809
PRIME MINISTER
1868–74, 1880–85,
1886, 1892–94
DIED Hawarden Castle,
Flintshire,
19 May 1898
AGE 88 years

Most people who are interested in politics begin by wanting to make great changes and then become more cautious as they grow older. William Gladstone did exactly the reverse. He started as a politician who rejected change and became someone with increasingly radical political views.

Gladstone made his name as Chancellor of the Exchequer from 1859–65, when he cut income tax and reduced government spending in order to promote prosperity and fairness. He supported working men's demands for the vote, and also the rights of non-conformists and Roman Catholics to worship freely. This brought him political success in 1868, when he became Prime Minister for the first time.

In office, he legalised trade unions, made improvements to the army and civil service, introduced secret ballots at elections, introduced a far-reaching education act, and disestablished the Anglican Church in Ireland, which meant it lost its official status. He also kept Britain out of any foreign wars. After he lost the 1874 election to Benjamin Disraeli and the Conservative Party, he retired from politics but returned in 1876 when he attacked the government for failing to protect the Bulgarians from persecution by their Ottoman Turkish rulers.

In 1880 he became Prime Minister again, ending a number of wars. However, his popularity fell when he failed to rescue the popular General Gordon from Khartoum, Sudan, and he resigned in 1885. This time he was out of office for less than a year, returning to power in 1886 with Irish Nationalist Party support. To keep that support, he introduced a bill to give home rule (self-government) to Ireland, but it was defeated in the House of Commons after his own party disagreed over the issue and he resigned.

In 1892 Gladstone was re-elected Prime Minister for the fourth time, but failed to get a new Irish Home Rule Bill through the House of Lords, finally resigning in 1894, at the age of 84.

Gladstone was a very moral person who believed strongly in individual freedom and thus thought that the government should interfere in peoples' lives as little as possible.

> Gladstone was known by his supporters as the 'Grand Old Man' or 'The People's William'.

He also believed in the rights of nations to govern themselves, hence his support for Irish nationalism, and did not support the growth of the British Empire. He therefore found himself increasingly out of touch with the British people, but did much to turn the Liberal Party into the major party of change in 19th-century British politics. 🏴

DAVID LLOYD GEORGE
'THE WELSH WIZARD'

BORN Manchester,
17 January 1863
PRIME MINISTER
1916–22
DIED Criccieth,
Gwynedd,
26 March 1945
AGE 82 years

Although he was born in Manchester, David Lloyd George was a Welsh-speaking Welshman, the only one ever to become Prime Minister. He was a brilliant and energetic war leader, steering Britain to victory in World War I in 1918.

Lloyd George trained as a solicitor and was elected Liberal member of parliament for Caernarfon Boroughs in 1890, a seat he held until 1945. He concentrated first on Welsh issues but also fiercely opposed the Boer War of 1899–1902. In 1905 the Liberals came to power and Lloyd George became President of the Board of Trade.

In 1908 Henry Asquith took over as Prime Minister and made Lloyd George Chancellor of the Exchequer. He introduced old age pensions in 1908 and National Insurance to provide benefits for unemployment, accident and sickness in 1911. To pay for these changes, he proposed new taxes on land and income which the House of Lords rejected. This led to the House of Lords being stripped of many of its powers in 1911, in order to get the taxes approved.

After war broke out in 1914, a joint Liberal-Conservative government took over in 1915. Lloyd George became

World War I

The increasing division of Europe in the early 1900s into two armed camps – with Britain, Russia and France on one side and Germany and Austria-Hungary on the other – led to war in 1914. During the war, huge numbers of men and amounts of materials were needed to gain victory.

Conscription – compulsory military service – was introduced in Britain in 1916, followed by food rationing in 1918. In the end, Britain and the USA, which joined the war in 1917, managed to out-produce and out-fight Germany, giving them victory in November 1918.

Minister of Munitions and, in 1916, Minister for War. In December 1916 he replaced Asquith as Prime Minister. He set up a war cabinet of five politicians to take all major political, military, economic and diplomatic questions, and proved to be a decisive and visionary war leader, unafraid of taking difficult decisions.

Soon after peace was declared in November 1918, Lloyd George and a coalition of Conservatives and Liberals won a major election victory. Although he helped to agree the 1919 Versailles Peace Treaty with the defeated Germany, and brought peace to Ireland in 1921, he failed to build the 'land fit for heroes to live in' that he had promised. He fell from power in 1922 but remained a member of parliament for the rest of his life. 🏴

> David Lloyd George was a charismatic and decisive leader who led Britain to victory in World War I.

WINSTON CHURCHILL
THE GREATEST BRITON

BORN Blenheim Palace, Oxfordshire, 30 November 1874
PRIME MINISTER 1940–45, 1951–55
DIED London, 30 January 1965
AGE 90 years

Many people consider Winston Churchill to be the greatest Briton who has ever lived. In 1940, when Britain faced almost certain defeat in its fight against Nazi Germany, Winston Churchill became Prime Minister and inspired the country to victory in 1945.

Churchill entered politics as a Conservative member of parliament in 1900 but changed sides to become a Liberal in 1904. He was to change political parties again in the future. During the Liberal government of 1906–15, he was President of the Board of Trade (1908), Home Secretary (1911) and First Lord of the Admiralty at the start of World War I (1914). However he was blamed for the disastrous decision to invade the Gallipoli peninsula in Turkey, at the cost of thousands of soldiers' lives, and resigned from the government in 1915, going off to fight in France.

He returned to the government as Minister of Munitions in 1917 and served in Lloyd George's peacetime government from 1918–22. He lost his seat in the 1922 general election but returned to parliament in 1924 and joined the Conservative government as Chancellor of the Exchequer. Churchill was not a great success as Chancellor, and during the 1930s he became increasingly isolated in parliament because of his opposition to Indian independence and his support for the unpopular Edward VIII, who abdicated (gave up his throne) in 1936.

However, Churchill was one of the first politicians to warn the country about Nazi Germany, and was the ideal candidate to become Prime Minister in 1940. The situation facing Britain was desperate, with Germany threatening to invade the country. In a series of great speeches, Churchill rallied the country behind him and threw all his efforts into winning the war. Although he sometimes made bad decisions, he was an inspiring war leader who alone stood up to Nazi Germany until Russia and the USA entered the war in 1941.

Winston Churchill giving one of his famous 'V for victory' hand signs.

Although Churchill led Britain to victory in May 1945, many people did not think he was the right person to lead them in peacetime, and he was heavily defeated by the Labour Party in the general election of July 1945. Churchill returned to power in 1951 but by then he was an old man and he finally retired from office in 1955, remaining in parliament until 1964, just three months before his death in January 1965.

CLEMENT ATTLEE
BRITAIN'S POST-WAR LEADER

BORN Putney, London,
  3 January 1883
PRIME MINISTER
  1945–51
DIED London,
  8 October 1967
AGE 84 years

Clement Attlee was a quiet man who led the Labour Party to a landslide victory in 1945. He became one of the most effective prime ministers Britain has ever had.

Many people consider Clement Attlee to be the most successful peace-time prime minister Britain has ever had.

Attlee was born into a well-off family and trained as a lawyer. He became a socialist after seeing at first hand the poverty and unemployment in the East End of London. In 1919 he became actively involved in politics as Labour Mayor of Stepney in East London and became its member of parliament in 1922. He gradually worked his way up the Labour Party, becoming leader in 1935, a position he held for 20 years.

In 1940 the Conservative government of Neville Chamberlain lost its power due to its terrible management of the war. Attlee led the Labour Party into the coalition (joint) government headed by Winston Churchill of the Conservative Party (see pages 40-41). Attlee was a loyal and able member of the war cabinet, chairing many important committees and becoming Deputy Prime Minister in 1942.

At the end of World War II in 1945, Winston Churchill called a general election, confident that his party would win. Many people, however, distrusted the Conservatives because of their poor record in power before the war, and voted in huge numbers for Attlee's Labour Party.

Once elected, Attlee's government set about taking industries, such as the railways, coal, gas and electricity, into public ownership, rebuilding the shattered economy, and setting up the

Attlee's ministers

Two men in Attlee's cabinet stand out for their skill and determination.

ERNEST BEVIN (1881–1951) was a former General Secretary of the Transport & General Workers' Union who became Foreign Secretary. He used his position to build a strong friendship between Britain and the USA and he supported the creation of NATO (the North Atlantic Treaty Organisation) with the USA and other western European states.

ANEURIN BEVAN (1897–1960) was a Welsh miner who became Minister of Health under Clement Attlee. He created the National Health Service, the first free-at-delivery health service in the world.

National Health Service. Abroad, he supported the rebuilding of Europe, led Britain into NATO, and above all, gave independence to India, Pakistan, Sri Lanka and Burma, starting the process of breaking up the British Empire.

Attlee's major achievement was to establish a model for running the country based on full employment, public and private companies, and a strong welfare state. This was accepted by all major political parties until the election of Margaret Thatcher in 1979.

MARGARET THATCHER
'THE IRON LADY'

BORN Grantham, Lincolnshire, 13 October 1925
PRIME MINISTER 1979–90

The only woman ever to have become Prime Minister, Margaret Thatcher was also the longest-serving Prime Minister since William Gladstone a century earlier. Her 11 years in office were not without trouble and she has continued to attract strong opinions ever since her retirement in 1990.

Margaret Roberts's father was a grocer who was active in local politics. She studied chemistry at Oxford University and worked as a research chemist before qualifying as a barrister. She married Denis Thatcher in 1951 and had twin children in 1953. First elected to parliament as a Conservative in 1959, she held junior posts in the government from 1961–64 and then became Education Secretary in Edward Heath's government of 1970–74.

After Heath lost two general elections in 1974, Margaret Thatcher challenged him for the leadership and won in 1975. When she made a speech critical of communist USSR in 1976, a Russian newspaper gave her the nickname the 'Iron Lady', in which she took great pride. In the 1979 general election, Margaret Thatcher led her party to victory. She tackled the economy by reducing the amount of money in circulation and putting up taxes. As unemployment rose above 3 million, she became hugely unpopular. However, when the Argentinians captured the Falkland Islands in the South Atlantic in 1982, she took decisive action to get the islands back, and won a landslide election victory in 1983.

Her second period as Prime Minister was marked by the year-long strike by the National Union of Miners against pit closures in 1984–85. Her government also sold off nationalised industries and reduced the role of the state in the economy. Millions of council houses were sold to their tenants, making many of them home-owners for the first time. As a result of these and other policies, the economy boomed. Abroad, she built up Britain's defences and formed close links with US President Ronald Reagan.

In 1987 Thatcher won a third election victory, but the economy struggled and a new flat-rate system of local taxation known as the community charge or 'poll tax', led to mass non-payment and rioting. As her popularity declined, her Deputy Prime Minister, Geoffrey Howe, resigned in 1990 in protest against her anti-European policies. This led to a leadership contest from which she withdrew after one round of voting.

Thatcher's legacy is still disputed, with many people claiming she rescued Britain from long-term economic decline, while others blame her for making the problems worse. She left a deeply divided Conservative Party, which, although it won again in 1992, lost heavily in 1997 and has yet to regain power.

Britain's only woman prime minister inspired both devotion and hatred during her 11 years in power.

Glossary

abdicate To give up the throne.

Act of Union Parliamentary act recognising the union of two countries.

Admiralty, First Lord of the Political head of the navy, often a member of the cabinet.

Anglican Church The official Protestant church in England, also known as the Church of England.

annul To make void a marriage.

ballot Act of voting by an elector using a marked ballot paper placed in a ballot box.

Board of Trade Government department responsible for trade and commerce, headed by the President.

cabinet Committee of senior government ministers chosen by the Prime Minister to advise him or her and to govern the country.

Catholic, Roman Christian who follows the authority of the Pope in Rome.

cavalry Soldiers who fight on horseback.

Chancellor of the Exchequer Government minister responsible for the country's finances, including the raising of revenue and its spending.

chronicle Record of events in chronological order.

civil war War between different peoples, parties or regions within the same country.

communism Belief in a society without different social classes in which everyone is equal and where all property is owned by the people.

consensus General or widespread agreement.

constitution Written document setting out principles on which a country is founded and how its people are to be governed.

coronation Formal, religious ceremony at which a monarch is crowned.

crusade Holy war undertaken for a religious cause.

democracy Government by the people or their elected representatives.

disestablishment Removal of official status from a national church.

Divine Right of Kings The belief that the king was divinely appointed and was answerable only to God for his actions.

empire Group of peoples or countries governed by one ruler.

general election Election in which every parliamentary constituency (seat) is fought at the same time.

heir to the throne Eldest son or daughter next in line to become king or queen.

Holy Land The area between the River Jordan and the Mediterranean Sea where most events in the Bible take place.

home rule Rule by the Irish parliament in Dublin.

Home Secretary Government minister responsible for law and order.

imperialist Person who supports an empire and its expansion to include other countries.

jubilee Special anniversary such as a 50th (golden) or 60th (diamond).

kingdom Country ruled by a monarch.

militia Body of citizens rather than professional soldiers, usually raised locally and used only in emergencies.

monarchy Country ruled by a hereditary king or queen.

munitions Military equipment and supplies, in particular ammunition.

nationalisation State ownership of an industry or service.

parliament Assembly of the representatives of a country which makes laws and holds the government to account; in England, an elected House of Commons and an unelected House of Lords.

pilgrimage Journey to a shrine or other religious places.

Prime Minister The first or main minister of the government, chosen by the monarch; at first, the informal title of the First Lord of the Treasury and only officially recognised in 1937.

Protestant Christian whose church broke away from the Roman Catholic Church during the Reformation of the 16th century, or was founded later.

ransom Money paid to release a captive or prisoner.

Reform Act Act of parliament reforming the electoral system.

reign Period during which the monarch rules the country.

republic Country governed by an elected head of state called a president.

royalist Person who believes in a government with a king or queen as head of state.

socialism Economic and social belief in equality and

co-operation rather than competition.

Tory Political group formed in the 1680s that supported the king and the established church; predecessor of the modern-day Conservative Party.

treason Course of action against or betrayal of a monarch or country.

treaty Formal and binding agreement between two or more countries, often to end a war between them.

tribe Group of people with a common descent or ancestor.

Whig Political group formed in the late 17th century that supported parliament and the Protestant succession to the throne; predecessors of the Liberal Party and modern-day Liberal Democrat Party.

Some useful websites

http://en.wikipedia.org/wiki/Main_Page
Wikipedia, the online encyclopedia, with entries for everyone mentioned in this book.

http://www.spartacus.schoolnet.co.uk/Britain.html
An online encyclopedia of British history.

http://www.royal.gov.uk/
The official website of the British monarchy.

http://www.bbc.co.uk/history/
The BBC history website.

Note to parents and teachers:
Every effort has been made by the Publishers to ensure that the websites in this book are suitable for children, that they are of the highest educational value, and that they contain no inappropriate or offensive material. However, because of the nature of the Internet, it is impossible to guarantee that the contents of these sites will not be altered. We strongly advise that Internet access is supervised by a responsible adult.

SOME PLACES TO VISIT

Houses of Parliament, London
The scene of many great debates and speeches in British history.

Buckingham Palace, London
Windsor Castle, Windsor, Berkshire
The two great royal residences.

Blenheim Palace, Woodstock, Oxfordshire
The palatial home of the Duke of Marlborough.

HMS *Victory*, Portsmouth, Hampshire
Horatio Nelson's flagship in dry dock at Portsmouth.

Osborne House, Isle of Wight
Queen Victoria's seaside retreat where she lived after Albert's death and where she died in 1901.

Chartwell, Westerham, Kent
Winston Churchill's country home from 1924 until his death in 1965.

Bannockburn, Stirling
The famous 1314 battle site.

Scone Palace, Perth
The abbey where all Scottish kings were crowned.

Caernarfon Castle, Gwynedd
Built by Edward I and the birthplace of the first Prince of Wales in 1284.

Index

These are the lists of contents for each title in *Great Britons*:

LEADERS
Boudica • Alfred the Great • Richard I • Edward I • Robert Bruce
Owain Glyndwr • Henry V • Henry VIII • Elizabeth I
Oliver Cromwell • The Duke of Marlborough • Robert Walpole
Horatio Nelson • Queen Victoria • Benjamin Disraeli
William Gladstone • David Lloyd George • Winston Churchill
Clement Attlee • Margaret Thatcher

CAMPAIGNERS FOR CHANGE
John Wycliffe • John Lilburne • Thomas Paine • Mary Wollstonecraft
William Wilberforce • Elizabeth Fry • William Lovett
Edwin Chadwick • Lord Shaftesbury • Florence Nightingale
Josephine Butler • Annie Besant • James Keir Hardie • Emmeline Pankhurst
Eleanor Rathbone • Ellen Wilkinson • Lord David Pitt • Bruce Kent
Jonathon Porritt • Shami Chakrabati

NOVELISTS
Aphra Behn • Jonathan Swift • Henry Fielding • Jane Austen
Charles Dickens • The Brontë Sisters • George Eliot • Lewis Carroll
Thomas Hardy • Robert Louis Stevenson • Arthur Conan Doyle
Virginia Woolf • D H Lawrence • J R R Tolkien • George Orwell
Graham Greene • William Golding • Ian McEwan • J K Rowling
Caryl Phillips • Andrea Levy • Zadie Smith
Monica Ali • Salman Rushdie

ARTISTS
Nicholas Hilliard • James Thornhill • William Hogarth
Joshua Reynolds • George Stubbs • William Blake • J M W Turner
John Constable • David Wilkie • Dante Gabriel Rossetti
Walter Sickert • Gwen John • Wyndham Lewis • Vanessa Bell
Henry Moore • Barbara Hepworth • Francis Bacon • David Hockney
Anish Kapoor • Damien Hirst

ENGINEERS
Robert Hooke • Abraham Darby • James Watt • John MacAdam
Thomas Telford • George Cayley • George Stephenson • Robert Stephenson
Joseph Paxton • Isambard Kingdom Brunel • Henry Bessemer
Joseph Bazalgette • Joseph Whitworth • Charles Parsons • Henry Royce
Nigel Gresley • Lord Nuffield • Harry Ricardo • Frank Whittle • Norman Foster

SCIENTISTS
John Dee • Robert Boyle • Isaac Newton • Edmond Halley • William Herschel
Michael Faraday • Charles Babbage • Mary Anning • Charles Darwin
Lord Kelvin • James Clerk Maxwell • Ernest Rutherford • Joseph Rotblat
Dorothy Hodgkin • Alan Turing • Francis Crick • Stephen Hawking
John Sulston • Jocelyn Bell Burnell • Susan Greenfield

SPORTING HEROES
WG Grace • Arthur Wharton • Kitty Godfree • Roger Bannister
Stirling Moss • Jackie Stewart • Bobby Moore • George Best
Gareth Edwards • Barry Sheene • Ian Botham • Nick Faldo
Torville and Dean • Lennox Lewis • Daley Thompson • Steve Redgrave
Tanni Grey-Thompson • Kelly Holmes • David Beckham • Ellen McArthur

MUSICIANS
William Byrd • Henry Purcell • George Frideric Handel • Arthur Sullivan
Edward Elgar • Henry Wood • Ralph Vaughan Williams • Noel Coward
Michael Tippet • Benjamin Britten • Vera Lynn
John Dankworth and Cleo Laine • Jacqueline Du Pre
Eric Clapton • Andrew Lloyd Webber • Elvis Costello
Simon Rattle • The Beatles • Courtney Pine • Evelyn Glennie